MERCY FOUND ME

Mary Elizabeth Edwards

DEDICATION

I would like to dedicate this book to my beautiful children: Michael, Elaine, Lashon, and Demetria. You are the expression of God's love toward me.

ACKNOWLEDGEMENTS

Special Acknowledgments To

My husband, Joe Edwards: you are my counselor, and my covering.

My parents, Louis and Julia Hayes: you have always been there for me.

My sons: Michael, Robert, Andrae; my daughters: Elaine, Lashon, Demetria, Lateish, Sanya, and Earline; and my grandchildren.

My sister, Loraine and Junior Thompson: for allowing me to stay at your home during my recovery; my sister, Lois McClam: for taking care of me; and to all of my siblings and in-laws for your love.

My cousins, Patricia and Gary White, and Vanessa Palmer; my nephew and niece, Lawrence and Karen Johnson.

My spiritual mother and mentor, Leola Payne.

My mother-in-law, Dorothy Edwards and Sarah Parham: you are my prayer warriors.

My aunt and godmother, Mary Brown.

All of my family and friends: thank you for your care and support.

TABLE OF CONTENTS

CHAPTER ONE

Jane Doe

I am a pastor's wife, proud mother, grandmother, daughter, sister, and friend. All of these roles are fulfilling and bring me happiness. I can truly say that I am a blessed woman. Loving people is not a hard thing for me to do. I show love because Jesus first loved me. I show others mercy because God and the ones I love have shown mercy to me when I needed it.

I tell you that her many sins are forgiven, so she showed great love. But the person who is forgiven only a little will love only a little (Luke 7:47 NCV).

A person who has been forgiven a lot usually forgives and loves a lot. And a person who is forgiven of little, normally doesn't show mercy toward other people. They often feel they have it all together, so everyone else should be the same.

Storms happen to everyone. Some may experience more than others, but storms still come to all of us. Our response to storms has a lot to do with how we treat people. We'll either treat them with compassion or indifference. You can easily tell what place you are responding from by your words and most importantly, your actions.

I'll be the first to say life is not always easy. Sometimes it's hard. Even in the hard places, you and I are left with the question, 'will I allow this to make me bitter or make me better?'

My experiences have made me better by the grace of God. Some people look at me and have no clue of where the Lord has brought me from. There is a popular phrase that says, 'I don't look like what I've been through.' That is truly my testimony.

This is why I decided to tell my story of how I went from being a rebellious teenager to the woman I am today. I know what it is to be raised in a God-fearing home to only find myself in a place of guilt, shame and suicide – much like the prodigal son in Luke 15:11-32. The amazing thing is my parents never gave up on me through it all.

As a result, I am committed to helping women and teenage children avoid some of the mistakes I made along the way. I have been on both ends of the spectrum as a teenager who thought my parents were too strict, to becoming a mother who wanted to protect my children with my own parenting style.

My goal is to build a bridge that will connect a relationship gap you might be experiencing between you and your child or you and your parent. Moms, you've probably said, "I've done all I can with this teenager of mine." And teenagers, you may feel like your parents don't know what they're talking about. They just don't understand you. I pray that you can find a reason to try again and never give up through the pages of my life.

God's goodness and mercy have always surrounded me as far as I can remember – but there are times when I know, beyond a shadow of a doubt, that mercy stood between me and death. Here is where my story with mercy begins.

Lost and Found

I was a church kid – raised and brought up in church. Back then, almost everything was considered a sin. You'd be on your way to hell for the smallest things. For example, let's say you wanted to go to the movies, dancing, swimming, or to a party. If you went, you'd definitely be hell-bound according to our elders. So, it's no surprise that I did not experience the prom or things that today's teenagers find common --- unless I snuck and went.

As I mentioned earlier, my parents taught me the way I should go. Though I heard the lessons they shared, something in me wanted to go my own way, do my own thing, and discover who I was through my own experiences – not through the rules given by anyone else. I was considered the rebellious child and always spoke my mind. Maybe I rebelled because my young mind did not understand my parents' heart of protection for me.

Most of my childhood was spent in New Jersey. I vividly remember a rainy, August night that changed my life forever. That was the night I finally stood up to my Dad about what I wanted to do (without sneaking out the house to do it). You see, it was my birthday and I had just turned eighteen. I could hardly wait to celebrate. I believed as most teenagers believe. That belief was, eighteen years old equals a grown adult. Nobody could or should tell me what to do, 'cuz I'm grown, right? At least that's what I thought.

I got all dressed up and ready to go out the door, when my Dad asked, "Where do you think you're going, young lady?"

"I'm going out," I replied.

"How are you getting ready to go out when that's not the rules of the house?"

"Dad," I exclaimed, "I make my own money. I have my own job. I will do what I want to do because I'm grown."

My Dad looked at me and said, "You're absolutely right. I have prayed for you, ministered to you, chastised you and you are still determined to do what you want to do. From this day forward, I am fully turning you over into the hands of the Lord."

I replied, "You can turn me to whoever you want to turn me over to because I'm going to do what I want to do. I want to go out, and I'm going right now."

That is exactly what I did. My cousin, Vanessa, and I left to go to the club. On our way, I decided to stop by a friend's house. My friend's mother asked where we were on our way to. I told her we were going out for a while. She immediately said, "You all don't need to go out tonight. You need to turn around and go home."

I believe God was sending me a warning through this lady like He sent a warning minutes prior through my Dad. I overrode God's message and told her, "No, we're going out tonight. Vanessa and I just bought our new outfits and I'm going to wear my outfit. We're going to the club."

The strange thing was a young man at the house began to talk to us and started saying things like there was no God, as if he was a devout atheist.

I don't recall how the conversation got to that point, but he was talking about God so negatively that it disturbed me.

Now, you know if I had an unsolicited response ready for my father, and my friend's mother – I definitely had one ready for this young atheist. I began my defense about God and His character to the man. Though he questioned the validity of my relationship with God (as I'd just defended my plans to go to the club a few breaths before), I still passionately told him that God was more real than anything that could be seen or touched. Nothing or nobody could convince me to believe differently.

Again, God forewarned me through the confrontation with my father (the first sign). He spoke again through my friend's mother (the second sign). Lastly, he used an atheist to question God's existence so that I could become a witness to him, and even myself (the third sign).

Warnings always come before destruction. When I missed the signs from people, God gave me another chance to draw the warning out of myself – with my own words. Maybe He thought if

I couldn't hear Him through someone else's voice, I'd be able to discern Him from my own voice.

There we were. Vanessa and I finally made it to the club, ready to party. It was a little dark in there, but I made my way to the dance floor. Less than five minutes later, I was shot by someone I did not know. I knew beyond a shadow of a doubt that I was hit by a bullet as I never felt pain like that before in my life. Out of all the people that were in the club that night, I was the only person shot. And the bullet was intended for the man I was dancing with. The first words out of my mouth was Lord Jesus.

For whosoever shall call upon the name of the Lord shall be saved (Romans 10:13 KJV).

I was calling Jesus so loud that everyone around me thought I was playing. I told them that I was shot, but they did not believe me. A group of people took me outside so they could really see what was going on with me. When I lifted my shirt, we saw where the bullet had already enlarged near my abdomen. Vanessa put her hand in my back and begin to call Jesus with me. That's when they saw that my back was full of blood.

I believe the Lord saved my life because I called on Him and I'd confessed His power to the atheist earlier that night. Even when I did not serve God like I should, I never denied Him. I also believe the prayers of my father had gone before me as a shield in the time of trouble.

The ambulance was called but they never came because they did not know how to get to the club location. But God still had a plan. He used one of my enemies to help me. She did not like me, and I did not like her. That still didn't stop the plan of God for my life.

The young lady got in the car with me, Vanessa, and the guy who drove us to the club. She gave directions on how to get to the hospital as she lived in the area. Had it not been for my enemy being at the right place, at the right time, I probably would not be alive today.

I was rushed into the hospital and placed on the examination table. The medical staff asked me my name. I could not tell them who I was because I had lost so much blood that I became unconscious. My family had not made it to the hospital at the time. So, I was officially given the name Jane Doe.

Jane Doe is a name given to a woman who is unknown or intentionally concealed. In medical terms, it is an unidentified patient admitted into the hospital. My name was Jane Doe during the emergency surgery and recovery. I was without an identity until my father and family made it to the hospital. It was my father that had to give the doctors my name and identity. Not only did my father tell them who I was, when I came to myself during recovery, my father told me who I was.

Who would have thought that the man I had a huge disagreement with hours before would be the same man who would have to tell me my name? My mother and father could have turned their back on me based on the way I'd acted toward them. Instead, they loved and supported me through my process of becoming.

I found out that people may write you off and label you as a nobody, or a Jane Doe, but you are somebody to God. And the Father has given you a name as a child of God. If you lose your way, remind yourself that the Lord knows your name and you belong to Him. He'll be there to comfort you and see you through every season of life.

The words of this song best sum up this part of my life:

Amazing Grace
How sweet the sound
That saved a wretch like me
I once was lost
But now I'm found
Was blind but now I see.

MERCY FOUND ME

CHAPTER TWO

A Father's Love

You will often hear me make reference to my parents. They gave me the foundation of who I am today. I did not understand everything about their decisions for me when I was young, but it all made sense as I got older.

I've learned that you will not always agree with your parents however, I believe it helps you understand them better when you know their heart. Most parents desire is to love, protect, and prepare their children on how to build a life of their own in the world. From time to time, there will be parents who are not good at showing love toward their child – not always because they're bad parents, but they might not know how to love due to unhealthy experiences they probably had in their childhood.

God blessed my siblings and me to have wonderful parents. I am writing this chapter a few days before Father's Day 2020. My father, Louis Oliver Hayes, passed away 17 years ago. I miss him just as much today as I did back then. My mind is filled with so many memories of Dad that still make me laugh, cry, and smile. Any person who met Bishop Louis Hayes would not soon forget him, if ever.

My Dad was the epitome of who and what a father is. God loved me so much that He blessed me with a man who is just as honorable and loving as my father – and that is my husband, Joe Lewis Edwards. In fact, my Dad prophesied to me about my husband coming into my life. I'll talk more about 'Edwards,' as he's affectionately called, more in the chapters to come. I'm beyond grateful to have/had such wonderful men in my life.

There are a lot of great qualities I could write to describe my husband and Dad as good

fathers, but I'd like to point out a few that I think
are ideal for men to pattern:

A Good Father is a Provider

He supplies everything his spouse and children
need. It's more than just a roof over our heads,
food to eat, and clothes to wear. A providing father
goes the extra mile to give his children financial,
and emotional support. There was a time when my
husband worked multiple jobs to provide for me
and our children. He sacrificed himself for us by
putting our needs in front of his own.

A Good Father is a Protector

He shields his family from harm or anything that
would threaten their safety. A protecting father
always has your back. My father was short in
stature, yet a giant in being there for his children
and grandchildren. We didn't have to ever worry
about feeling safe. My family felt safe through my
father's protection – sometimes the protection
came through prayer and advice about life.

A Good Father is Present

He does his best to be a part of his child's life with
his presence. A lot of times a child would rather
have your attention and time rather than gifts. You

are able to see what is going on in your child's world when you are 'all there.' Being a present father gives a chance to build a personal relationship of trust with your child – so that he or she can feel comfortable coming to you about anything.

A Good Father is Persistent
He never gives up on his children. A persistent father loves unconditionally, even if his child goes astray. Love is the driving force behind all he does, and family is first. My husband and my father have always kept family as top priority. Their love remained the same through good and bad times. The Scripture says love is patient, kind, and longsuffering.

Love is very patient and kind, never jealous or envious, never boastful or proud; never haughty or selfish or rude. Love does not demand its own way. It is not irritable or touchy. It does not hold grudges and will hardly even notice when others do it wrong. It is never glad about injustice but rejoices whenever truth wins out.

If you love someone, you will be loyal to him no matter what the cost. You will always believe in him, always

expect the best of him, and always stand your ground
in defending him (I Corinthians 13: 4-7 TLB).

The Prodigal Son

A wonderful picture of this kind of love is found in Luke 15:11-32. Jesus tells a story about a father's youngest son coming to him to ask for inheritance ahead of time. The son takes his inheritance and wasted it on partying, prostitutes, friends, and anything else he could think of – until his money ran out. When the money runs out, the friends usually run out. It got so bad for the young man that he took a job feeding pigs.

I can imagine how he must have felt; to go from a penthouse to a pig house, just because of one wrong decision. The prodigal son probably felt worthless, ashamed, and maybe even stupid because of his actions. But I like where this story takes a turn. The Bible says the son finally came to himself. He had a moment where he could think straight and rationally.

When he finally came to his senses, he said to himself, 'At home even the hired men have food enough and to spare, and here I am, dying of hunger! I will go home to my father and say, "Father, I have sinned against both heaven and you, and am no longer worthy of being called your son. Please take me on as a hired man" (Luke 15:17-19 TLB).

The enemy created an illusion in the son's mind to make him believe that he was missing out on life or maybe his father didn't want him to have any fun. I believe this illusion was meant to build a hedge between the son and his father. One of Satan's goals is to cause a relationship divide to separate a child from his father's covering. If he can isolate the child from his parent's voice of wisdom, immature mistakes are bound to happen. Eventually one bad decision leads to another until life spins out of control.

Thank God the prodigal son re-gained control by first coming to his senses. His next step was deciding to go home and make it right with his father. As the son was approaching home, he probably didn't know that his father saw him coming from a far distance. This meant the father had been watching and waiting for his son's return for, who knows how long.

One thing is for sure – mercy found the young son that day. The father could have chosen punishment for what his son deserved but instead, the father showed him mercy and compassion.

The same way the father waited and had mercy on his son is the same way The Father waits and has mercy on you and me. There is nothing so bad that you've done that God won't forgive. Even if you have drifted far from Him, He is there watching and waiting for your return back home. But you must always keep a repentant heart. The psalmist David once prayed a simple prayer that says, 'create in me a clean heart and renew a right spirit within me.'

When you have a repentant spirit, something changes within you. You change your mind and actions into doing what you know is right. God can work with a contrite and humble spirit. I want you to walk away from this chapter remembering a few qualities of a good father. They are identical to some of the characteristics of God, the Father: our protector, provider, who is present and persistent.

Fathers, continue to be those things to your children and show them mercy when they need it. You are not optional in our society. You are a necessity in our homes, communities and our world. Just as I celebrate the wonderful father my husband and Dad have been, I also celebrate all the good fathers who are doing right by their children and families.

For fathers who may not be present in your child's life, I encourage you to just try. You don't have to be a perfect father, just try and start where you are to be in your child's life. God will never give up on you, so please never give up on your children. Keep working with them until they get it. That's what my father did for me.

The love of my natural father ran me into the love of my Heavenly Father. You and I must strive to show the love of God to everyone we meet. We may be the only picture of love some may ever see. Show mercy and kindness to others whenever you can. You never know when you'll need that same mercy to be given back to you.

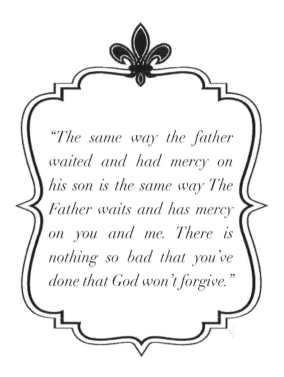

"The same way the father waited and had mercy on his son is the same way The Father waits and has mercy on you and me. There is nothing so bad that you've done that God won't forgive."

CHAPTER THREE

The Well

Have you ever had a taste for something to eat, only to find you're still not satisfied after you have eaten it? Nine times out of ten, your body is probably more thirsty than hungry. There are some physical cravings and thirsts that can only be satisfied by pure water. In fact, the human body can survive without food longer than it can without water.

The younger generation is more likely to drink juice and soda before water. It's been said that the human body is made up of around 60% water for adults. As you can see, water is very important for our lives. Some of the benefits of drinking water are: it carries oxygen to cells, it flushes out toxins in our body through urine, and it lubricates our joints.

Thirst is a broad word that is associated with a craving. It does not always refer to a natural or physical sense. Sometimes you can be thirsty for love, success, attention, or a deeper relationship with God. These things aren't seen with the physical eye, but they are just as real as a bottle of water you hold in your hand. Inner thirst can show up through your relationships and even your health.

If you are in and out of relationships a lot, you may be thirsty for love. If a conversation has to always be centered around you, you might be thirsty for attention. If there is a struggle with substance abuse, it could be a thirst for healing or a closer walk with the Lord.

There is a woman in the Bible who experienced inner thirst just like you and me. I'll begin by saying thirst isn't a bad thing. What makes it good or bad is determined by what source the thirst is connected to.

THE WELL

Now Jacob's well was there. Jesus therefore, being wearied from his journey, sat thus by the well. It was about the sixth hour. A woman of Samaria came to draw water. Jesus said to her, Give me a drink (John 4:6-7 NKJV).

Jesus was tired from his journey and decided to stop and rest at a well. I don't know how long he sat at the well, but I know it was long enough for Him to come in contact with the Samaritan woman, Photine. Jesus could have spoken to many people that day at the well; however, I am convinced He had a divine appointment with Photine. She probably never imagined that one trip to draw water would change her entire life. As Jesus sat at the well, the Samaritan woman came to draw water. Jesus started a conversation and asked her for a drink of water. Photine was surprised that Jesus would even talk to a Samaritan because He was Jewish. (Jews and Samaritans had no dealings with each other).

Jesus said, "If you knew who you were talking to, you would ask me for a drink of living water." He explained that if she drank water from the well, she'd get thirsty again; but if she drank from the living water that He gives, she'd never thirst again.

Living Water

When we talk about anything 'living', it means the present, this moment, right now. Living water has the power to deal with any right now situation. He offers a drink of living water every day through His Word to deliver you from trouble. It's up to you to accept or reject His invitation. When you receive Jesus into your heart, you will discover the purpose of God for your life, just like the Samaritan woman did.

For I know the thoughts I think toward you, says the LORD, thoughts of peace and not of evil, to give you a future and a hope, says the Lord. (Jeremiah 291:11 NKJV)

THE WELL

The Lord had a bigger plan for Photine's life – that's why I believe he sat and waited on her. He had need of her and she had need of Him. Jesus needed her water for his physical thirst and Photine needed the living water He had for her spiritual thirst.

Many people focus on Jesus as a Savior from sins. But He was just as much a prophet as He was a Savior during His ministry on earth. He told her about the man she was currently living with and the five husbands she'd already had. Jesus' prophecies were a little different than the prophecies we hear today. Some prophets today can only see houses and cars, but Jesus sees the real you.

The Samaritan woman's past and present was a little messy, yet He still had a bright future for her. Photine's story did not end at the well. The well was where her new life ministry just got started.

After Photine's encounter with Jesus, she ran home to tell her family and friends that she met the Messiah who told her all she had done. Her testimony was so impactful that many of the Samaritans in the city received salvation, off of the testimony of this one woman.

Photine became what we call a traveling evangelist. It's been said that she preached the message of Jesus Christ to anyone who would listen. Some writers suggest she carried the gospel from Samaria to parts of Africa, and even Rome. She was willing to die for the sake of the gospel – and she did.

The Samaritan and her family suffered great persecution for their faith. The Roman Emperor threw her in the bottom of a dry well to die after she refused to offer sacrifices to his gods. Photine kept the faith and finished her course in a well much like Jacob's well, where she met Jesus for her first drink of living water. As the Samaritan crossed over from time to eternity, she received her just reward as Jesus promised – water that sprang up into everlasting and eternal life.

The Whole Person

I understand why Jesus waited at the well for this woman. He already knew the impact her life would have for the kingdom of God. She probably did not look like much in the eyes of people before she met Christ, but God has a way of turning our mess into a message.

Notice the way Jesus ministered to her. In John 4:16, He told her to go and bring her husband (speaking about her present situation). Jesus also told her she had five husbands (speaking about her past). Lastly, He shared that if she drank of the water He gives, she will never thirst again (speaking of the future).

God wants to minister to your whole person – your past, present, and your future. You have been made to be the carrier of living water. In fact, you are a well. The Lord will send people to you to draw water (so they can drink) from your well -- a well of wisdom, well of encouragement, a well of direction, a well of mercy, and a well of love.

You will have many 'well experiences' in your life. God will send people to your well or send you to another person's well so you can get a drink. These encounters are divine appointments orchestrated by God.

One of my favorite things to do is decorate and design for events. When people come to an event, they see finished decorations, center pieces, and flowers. What they don't see is everything that goes on behind the scenes. There are a lot of moving pieces and moving parts that have to happen to organize the event.

This is how divine appointments work. God orchestrates time, people, and things to bring about His will. Our job is to be open to His leading and His voice. If you don't remember anything else I've written in this chapter, remember that God loves you and has need of you. It doesn't matter how far you've gotten away from God. He is waiting on you to choose Him because He has already chosen you.

Stay open and look for Him in your everyday life. Divine opportunities are all around you. You just have to be open to receive them. Just like the Samaritan woman, we all have a choice to accept or reject Jesus in our lives. Be sensitive to His leading. Jesus can meet you at church. He can meet you at the store. Or, He may even decide to meet you at the well.

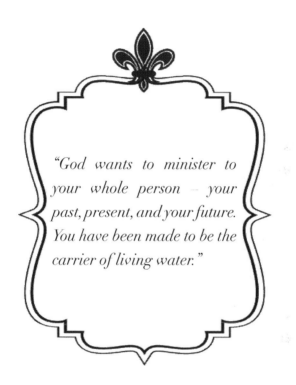

"God wants to minister to your whole person – your past, present, and your future. You have been made to be the carrier of living water."

CHAPTER FOUR

Hear My Prayer

O God, you have declared me perfect in your eyes; you have always cared for me in my distress; now hear me as I call again. Have mercy. Hear My Prayer. (Psalms 4:1 The Living Bible).

Some people believe that God doesn't hear a sinner's prayer. I do not believe that way. My life experiences show that God hears a sincere prayer – whether it's from a saint or sinner. He heard me and delivered me time and time again when I was out of fellowship with Him. The Bible says that the Lord rains on the just as well as the unjust (Matthew 5:45). It even says that He is married to the backslider. This means He is committed to loving us no matter what.

My husband and I just celebrated our 37th wedding anniversary a week ago. We have seen each other at our best and worst and are still happily married after all these years. Edwards and I get on each other's nerves sometimes, but 'he ain't going nowhere and I ain't either.' As committed as we are to our marital vows, God is even more committed about His vow of never forsaking His children. It is possible for us to leave Him, but He won't ever leave us.

The best way I can describe this kind of commitment is with two words – unconditional love. It doesn't take into account the wrong that has been done. God loves you because He is love itself. When you come to Him with a sincere heart and a sincere prayer, He will hear you; even if you feel you're not worthy of love as I did a long time ago.

Rock Bottom

I reached a place in my life where I felt I was as low as I could go in my young adult years. This was probably the darkest of days I had ever experienced. I even contemplated suicide. It moved from contemplation to an actual suicide attempt.

I didn't think my children, parents, or anyone loved me because it seemed like I messed up my entire life beyond repair. I figured death might be easier than trying to live. So, I decided to carry out my plan.

I went to a liquor store and purchased a bottle of MD 20/20. I drank it along with a bottle of Tylenol aspirin. I was so far gone that I got in the car and put my foot to the metal; driving as fast as the car would allow. I ran through every red light on Sunrise Boulevard. If anyone is familiar with Sunrise Boulevard in South Florida, they already know that it's an extremely busy street.

I drove until I wound up on the side of the road completely out of gas. The effects of the liquor and pills had me almost unconscious as my body slumped over the steering wheel. The constant sound of the horn filled the air that surrounded me. I will never forget the man that came to my car and tapped on the window.

He said, "Ma'am, ma'am, are you okay?"

I replied, "Yes," with very slurry speech.

"Where are you trying to get to," he asked.

"Just take me to my job. Help me get back to my job."

And he did. When I got inside my workplace, I told my boss what I could recall, and he immediately called the ambulance. After the medical team evaluated me, they determined it was too late for me to be taken to the hospital to have my stomach pumped. I believe I should have been taken to the hospital since this was a suicide attempt. Instead, the medical supervisor called my parents to come pick me up and take me home.

I stayed shut in the room for a week before I could fully grasp what happened to me. I knew I should have died based on the amount of substance in my body. God just wouldn't let it be so. He did not even allow any cars to hit me while speeding down the highway. He kept His angels shielding and protecting me each mile of the way. As far as the young man who stopped to help me on Sunrise Boulevard – I never saw him again. He very well could have been an angel. The Bible tells us not to forget to entertain strangers because some may be angels unaware.

I've known Him to be a way maker and a miracle worker when I was able to pray for myself and when I wasn't consciously able to pray. You can reach a point where you may not be able to pray in an audible way. In times like these, the Spirit of God and the prayers of the righteous make intercession on your behalf.

We don't always know what to pray for or why we pray for certain things or people. You can be sure that you are a product of somebody's prayer. It could be the prayers of your parents, grandparents, or a total stranger that has kept you this far.

MERCY FOUND ME

There's an old congregational song that says:

Somebody prayed for me
They had me on their mind
They took the time and prayed for me
I'm so glad they prayed
I'm so glad they prayed
I'm so glad they prayed for me

You and I should ask the Lord to give us a praying spirit every day. Luke 18:1 says, "Men ought to always pray, and not faint." If you don't know what to pray, consider praying for mercy; mercy for the world, your family, and yourself. There is a time for justice and there is a time of mercy. Mercy is a cry to God to give you another chance.

No one will get everything right 100% of the time. At some point, you will need grace and mercy to show up in your life. This is why I think it's important to show compassion to others -- because you don't know when you and your family will need it. In fact, your family may need it the most; especially your children and grandchildren. It's a given that they are going to make mistakes, just like you and I did growing up. But don't give up on them. Keep praying and working with them until they get it.

Pray that God gives them people for their life. Pray that they'll be kept from evil. Pray God's favor and protection over them. And most importantly, pray that God would save them and use them for His glory all the days of their lives.

Remember, God hears a sincere prayer. It doesn't have to be loud and doesn't have to have a lot of words. The length of your prayer does not mean it is more powerful. For example, the thief that hung on the cross next to Jesus in Luke 23:42-43 prayed a sincere prayer of nine words that changed his eternal destiny:

"Jesus, remember me when you come into your kingdom." Jesus immediately answered his prayer with thirteen words, "Today shalt thou be with me in paradise. This is a solemn promise."

God still answers prayers. He may not come based on your timetable, but He will be right on time. All you need is proof that He's made a way for you at least one time in your life. If He did it before, He can do it again. Keep praying, trusting and believing Him to work miracles through your prayers.

CHAPTER FIVE

What I Needed Most

I cannot stress how important prayer is to have a successful life. Communication with God is what will keep you strong in difficult times. Prayer is not just an adult thing or what older people do. Children can also pray and receive a blessing from the Lord.

If you want to hear prayers that are filled with purity and hope, ask a child to pray. They will usually speak from the innocence of their heart. My children's prayers and desire for me to get saved is what made me give my life completely to the Lord.

The Turning Point

My rock bottom phase felt like I'd never make it out. I saw no end in sight, yet the Lord heard the petition of my children to help me make a decision to change my life. Any major decision can be traced back to a day, place, and time. And I remember this one so well.

A dear friend invited me to church one Sunday morning. It was missionary day. I decided to go even though I was a 'little tipsy' that day. I went inside the church and sat near the back as to not be seen or draw any attention to myself. Bishop Payne was up ministering at the time. All of a sudden, he looked at me and called me to the front. He said, "The Lord wants to do something for you today."

Bishop used wisdom and asked all my children to come up to the front with me. He asked them "What do you want the Lord to do for your mom today?" Without hesitation, they said, "We want the Lord to save our momma." In that moment I thought, oh my God, my kids do love me. They do want me in their lives.

That was a breakthrough moment because I thought they would not love me due to the mistakes I made as a parent during the most important formative years of their life. They could have chosen differently, but they chose to love me through it instead. For that, I am so thankful. I experienced the love of God through my children that Sunday morning. And I have been running for Jesus ever since. I can honestly say their prayers, love, and care healed my soul as a mother.

The Best in the World

I have the best children in the whole world. It is natural instinct for parents to protect their children. It is an even greater blessing to have children who have a heart to protect their parents. God has blessed me with four wonderful children who I am extremely proud of.

My first born is my son, Michael. If you meet him for the firtime, you will immediately gravitate to him. My son has a loving and giving heart toward people. He will do anything in his power for anybody in need. I love that about him. You will not find a greater giver and supporter who will be with you through thick and thin. I could not have asked the Lord for a better son. God gave me His best in the person of my only begotten son, in whom I am well pleased.

My next child is my daughter, Elaine. She is like the mother figure of my children. Elaine is the glue that keeps the family together. She has a heart of gold and is the greatest encourager and cheerleader. I admire what an awesome wife, mother, daughter and sister she is. Elaine is the gift that keeps on giving. When God made Elaine, He threw the mold away because she is truly one of a kind.

Lashon is my next oldest daughter. She has always been my quiet and shy child. Lashon has always been the one to stay up under me. I never knew she had such a big voice to sing until I heard her at church. I love that Shon has always had a heart for the things of God. Her passion, loyalty to God, and her creative abilities are second to none.

My youngest is my daughter, Demetria. I so admire her determination. She has been a go-getter since a child. Demetria learned her numbers and ABCs at a very young age; so, it's no surprise that she has accomplished so much in the field of education. When Demetria makes up her mind to do something, she lets nothing or no one stand in her way to reach her goal. I wouldn't be surprised if she ends up being the mayor of the city she lives in. Her leadership ability has always been there and will continue to take her far.

Don't Count Me Out

Who would have ever thought that God would allow broken pieces of my life to produce such a masterpiece through my children. If you go off of statistics alone, my children could have easily been labeled as the least likely to be anyone great – but God. Because of Him and their perseverance to overcome any odds that may have been against them, they have all done well in life.

I think it goes to show that we shouldn't count anyone out – especially if their circumstances may look different than the typical family dynamics. These are the cases where God specializes most. For every single mother or father reading this book, your story does not have to be surrounded by guilt and shame from things of your past. You can begin again from where you are right now.

Ask the Lord to help you to make the best decisions for you and your children. Your relationship with God and your relationship with your children are the most important things to focus on in re-building or maintaining a balanced life. The Lord will help you just like He helped me. Allow God to take the driver seat in your life. Nobody knows you better than He does. If you surrender all to Him, He'll give you just what you need the most.

"Your story does not have to be surrounded by guilt and shame from things of your past. You can begin again from where you are right now."

CHAPTER SIX

Relationships

The main ingredients of a family unit are God, communication, respect, and right priorities. It can be very hard to maintain healthy relationships within your home if Jesus is not at the center. When you seek to please Him first, and make your spouse and children top priorities, it lessens the chance of having a broken home. There's no guarantee that homes won't ever break up even if you do the things I just mentioned – but again, it can lessen the chances.

Everyone's home relationship is different. What works for one family may not work exactly the same for another. You have to find what works best for you and your family based on the Word of God. The Bible is full of wisdom on how to raise your children.

For example, Proverbs 22:6 says, "Train up a child in the way he should go and when he is old, he will not depart from it." The Message version says, "Point your kids in the right direction – when they're old, they won't be lost." This means when we do our best to teach our children right from wrong, they'll choose the right path when they get grown.

My parents taught all their children the ways of God. And the Scripture has been fulfilled in our lives as we are all serving the Lord and involved in ministry some kind of way. Mom and Dad showed us how a husband should love his wife and a wife submit to her husband. Their love was something for everyone to pattern.

Fathers are the first picture a little girl has to show her how she should be treated by men. They are also the first example for boys in teaching them how to treat young girls and women. It's been said that you can always tell how a man will treat you by how he treats his mother. If he respects his mother or the woman that raised him, nine times out of ten he'll respect you. Most young girls dream of one day finding their prince charming. Many grow up and find that their dream came true. Others woke up to a relationship that was nothing short of a nightmare.

<u>From A Nightmare to A Dream</u>

Being a single mother is not easy. Being in a toxic, abusive relationship multiplies hardship and pain. Add drugs and alcohol use to a relationship – heartbreak is bound to happen. I was in an abusive relationship when I was out of fellowship with the Lord. I knew that relationship was not good for me and I knew that it was not real love. Love is not supposed to hurt. It does no harm. The question people ask women in abusive relationships is, why did you stay? Why didn't you just leave? I think the reason is because of fear.

A lot of women fear for their lives and the ones they love. When fear is used to control a person, threats are taken very seriously because you just don't know if the threats will be acted upon.

Domestic violence or relationship abuse is when one partner maintains power over the other partner through behavioral patterns. Some of these patterns and warning signs are:

- Looks at you in a threatening way
- Demeans and criticizes you
- Intimidates you with weapons
- Tells you you're un-loveable
- Shows extreme jealousy of you being with family/friends
- Threatens to hurt you, your children, or family
- Prevents you from having access to bank accounts
- Abandons you in unfamiliar places

There are many more signs to look for as there are different types of relationship abuse. Most are familiar with physical abuse because bruises are easier to see. Emotional abuse may be harder to identify since it affects the inner part of a person. Abuse in any form can take a toll on you --- especially how it has an effect on the relationship with yourself, family, and potential mates in the future.

The abuse I endured in a relationship made me think that I would never find someone to love me the way I desired to be loved. But one day, my father prophesied to me, a husband. He said, "Tiny, if you stay with the Lord this time, God is going to give you a wonderful husband who will love you. And you won't have to worry about anything." As I've shared in a prior chapter, Dad was a man of wisdom and often gave me the advice and encouragement I needed.

A Blessing in Disguise

I've always prayed that I would marry a man who'd be just like my Dad – someone who loved God, had a heart for people, who'd be a great provider, and would love my children. My father's example gave me a clear picture of what I could one day have in a husband. Dad gave me hope that my knight in shining armor would come into my life. And my father was right. My abusive relationship ended, I gave my life to the Lord and then met a wonderful man named, Joe Lewis Edwards, in a short amount of time.

Edwards, as I affectionately call him, was a young minister that I met at a church service. I really liked that he was a gentleman, tall, and had a warm personality. Practically, everyone around us was in support of our new-found relationship, seeing how my life was changing for the better.

I know, beyond any doubt, that it was the purpose and will of God for my husband and I to be together. That's why we married within three months of dating. On average, I would encourage single ladies and men to give yourself some time to heal from your last relationship before getting involved with another one. The reason I suggest waiting a while is because you may need to deal with or bring closure to any issues you may have experienced from the previous relationship. Relationships are a lot of work but it's worth it when you have someone who loves you as much as you do them. It's the same for marriage.

Marriage is a beautiful thing when you do it God's way with the right person. It requires patience, kindness, forgiveness, love, and mercy. You should try to look for ways to be a blessing to one another. Singles, if you desire a mate, don't lose hope. Just pray and ask God to send you someone who lines up with His will. If you have children, consider looking for someone who will love your children as if they are his or her own.

That's exactly what happened with Edwards and me. My husband does not have any biological children of his own, yet he's always loved my children as if they came from him. He is a wonderful father and grandfather in every way.

I went from a toxic, nightmare relationship to meeting the man of my dreams. For 37 years we've lived happily ever after. Don't give up on love. It has a way of finding you when you least expect it.

CHAPTER SEVEN

A Thanksgiving Miracle

There is a central theme that has been present throughout my life. If I had to sum it up in five words, it would be "God's mercy and divine intervention." In other words, I am a miracle. A miracle is an unexplainable event that takes place by divine intervention. It overrides natural and physical laws.

Miracles happen every day. The ability to go to sleep and wake up the next day is a miracle. It's easy to take it for granted because we usually expect it to happen day by day without any thought. God's hand of protection that keeps you and your family safe is a miracle. The placement of the sun, moon, and stars is a miracle. The way God designed the body to function on its own is also a miracle.

If you happen to get a small cut in your finger, it will heal on its own after a few days to a week. The body was designed to repair and heal itself. It may not always heal itself quickly due to other underlying issues but in general, our bodies are one of God's miraculous creations.

I have had some health challenges, big and small, along the way; but the Lord has kept and delivered me through them all. Again, if He's done it for me, He will do it for you. I keep sharing personal testimonies with you to inspire you to believe and trust God when it seems you can't trace Him.

<u>Someone Had to Die</u>

It is almost hard to believe that it's been almost nine years since I had a liver transplant. This experience was unlike anything I'd ever faced before. For those who know about organ transplants, it can usually take a year or longer before finding a good match. I desperately needed a new liver. In order for me to get a liver meant that someone would have to die and be listed as an organ donor. I was only on the waiting list for three months when others had been waiting longer than I.

On Thanksgiving night, I received a call that I needed to get to the hospital right away. I thought someone was playing a prank on the phone, so I hung up. The person called again and said that they found a match for my liver and I needed to go to the hospital to have the transplant surgery done.

I was shaking like a leaf because the call caught me by surprise. I had to take a few minutes to calm myself. Afterwards, I packed my bag and headed to the hospital. I later found out that a young girl had just passed away in Miami from a car accident and I would be receiving her liver for my transplant.

You never want to hear of anyone dying, especially any one young. Young people have not had a chance to live and see what the world is about. The thought that her life was cut short was really sad. I had to accept that when she lost her life, she saved mine. My sister, Lois, and I prayed that God would save her soul and receive her to

Himself. I cannot imagine the pain her parents felt that night and are probably still feeling to this day. I don't think a parent ever gets over losing a child. Only God can heal that kind of hurt.

Someone had to die so another person might live. Someone had to give their life so someone else could live. I know I'm repeating myself, but I want to make a point. The experience I shared with this precious, young girl gives us a snapshot of the cross. Jesus had to die so that we could have eternal life. He exchanged His life for ours because He loved us just that much.

Jesus asked the Father if there was any other way because of all that He had to endure to redeem us. This was the only way. Death was the only door that led to life. Jesus had you and me on His mind as He hung on the cross. He stayed there and sacrificed His life because He thought we were worth it.

<u>The Process of the Transplant</u>

A transplant of any kind has to do with removing an organ or tissue from one place to put it in another. In my case, the young girl's liver was removed from her body to be placed in mine. Some transplants go smoothly as planned and others have some bumps in the road.

My liver transplant surgery went fine, and I was released to go home. After being home a week or so, I started to experience complications like dizziness, vomiting, and fatigue. I felt so bad that I passed out. That's when my daughter, Lashon, called the ambulance to take me back to the hospital. The doctors ran several tests and concluded that my body had begun to resist the liver. And things took a turn for the worst.

I was surrounded by prayers, love and support from my husband, children and family though I knew this was a battle that only God and I could fight. I looked at myself in the mirror and saw how dark my skin had become. I thought I looked like a monster. My body literally shed skin day by day. There was a moment when it seemed that I looked at death face to face. I had to decide whether I was going to fight for my life or give in to the circumstances I saw in the natural. I decided to live. I made a deliberate decision to speak to my liver and command it to function the way it was designed to function.

Yes, there were days when things looked contrary to my confession. That was the time I had to hold on to God's promise even stronger. I found it important to keep praise music, Scriptures, positive people and positive thoughts ever before me. When you go through test and trials, you have to have people that will speak faith along with you. Their faith will help you stay strong on days you might feel weak. I can't thank God enough for those He has placed in my life.

After a while, my liver started lining up with my confessions. I knew my story could not end there because I had more that God wanted me to do. I also knew that I wanted to live to see and enjoy my children, grandchildren, and one day, great-grandchildren. (I now have one great-grand child and one on the way).

I have not had any other problems with my liver ever since. That was a Thanksgiving I will never forget. This miracle working God we serve does all things well and I give Him all the glory for it. Don't give up on miracles. They can still happen if you stay fully persuaded that God will do what He promised. We'll close this chapter with how Abraham received his miracle from God in

Romans 4:18-21 (The Living Bible):

So, when God told Abraham that he would give him a son who would have many descendants and become a great nation, Abraham believed God even though such a promise just couldn't come to pass. And because his faith was strong, he didn't worry about the fact that he was too old to be a father at the age of one hundred, and that Sarah his wife, at ninety, was also much too old to have a baby.

But Abraham never doubted. He believed God, for his faith and trust grew ever stronger, and he praised God for this blessing even before it happened. He was completely sure that God was well able to do anything He promised.

We have to be like Abraham with our faith by believing God beyond what we see. Feed your faith every day until your faith grows strong. Lastly, praise God for the miracle before it happens. Expect your miracle today!

CHAPTER EIGHT

Don't Give Up

The only way to know God as a Restorer is to experience loss. Maybe you have lost a spouse, job, or even your self-worth – I encourage you to keep pushing forward and never give up. I've done my best to show how mercy, perseverance, and determination can cause a breakthrough to the other side. It does not matter how bad a situation may be. God will either bring you out of it or give you the grace to handle what you're dealing with.

For this thing I besought the Lord thrice, that it might depart from me. And he said unto me, My grace is sufficient for thee: for my strength is made perfect in weakness. Most gladly therefore will I rather glory in my infirmities, that the power of Christ may rest upon me.

Therefore I take pleasure in infirmities, in necessities, in persecutions, in distresses for Christ's sake: for when I am weak, then I am strong (2 Corinthians 12:8-10 KJV).

The Living Bible translation says, "Three times I begged God to make me well again. Each time he said, No. But I am with you; that is all you need. My power shows up best in weak people." You don't have to always have to be strong. I don't think that it is humanly possible to be strong all the time. The Scripture you just read lets you know that you can exchange your weakness for God's strength any time you need it. And most importantly, take courage in knowing that God is with you.

When you know God is with you, you can outlast every storm. It can even boost your confidence. What if you and I approached each day with the knowing that the creator of heaven and earth is with us? If we really take a hold of this truth, we would have no reason to fear. The Psalmist wrote, "The Lord is my light and my salvation; whom shall I fear? The Lord is the strength of my life; of whom shall I be afraid? (Psalms 27:1 KJV).

The enemy has a plan to try to destroy anyone who is full of purpose. The Word of God promises that if evil comes to destroy you and me, it will stumble and fall because God will rescue His children. Our job is to be open to receive the Lord's help even when it looks different than what we'd expected. He knows what's best for us and He knows what lies ahead.

My purpose for writing this book is to testify of the mercies of God that has sustained my life. Secondly, I want to tell everyone reading to not give up, especially in the following areas:

1. Don't give up on God.

2. Don't give up on your family/children.

3. Don't give up on love.

4. Don't give up on miracles.

5. Don't give up on yourself.

Give Yourself Grace

As we are in the middle of this pandemic, I believe it is important to give grace. I've shared a lot about being compassionate with others, but I'd like to end this book about showing yourself grace. We can sometimes be our worst critic. The same mercy we extend to others is the same mercy we should give to ourselves.

You are doing well as long as you keep trying. You will have lost the battle the moment you decide to quit. There's one thing I've learned from my father and mother's life – quitting is not an option. When my father went home to be with the Lord 15+ years ago, my mother could have easily decided to stop living and go home to be with the Lord. On March 3rd 2020, she celebrated her 96th birthday and is still kicking!

It's almost impossible to give up and throw in the towel after coming from such a rich heritage that Bishop Louise and Mother Julia Hayes has birthed. Because of them, the Hayes Family is one of promise and great legacy. It flows from them, to their children, grandchildren, great-grandchildren, and generations to come.

No matter how many times we may fall, we always get back up again, stronger than we were before. I am who I am because God loved me and my parents loved me. I am alive today because God remembered the prayers they prayed for me.

They did not quit so neither can I. Regardless of what family you come from, give yourself a chance to do your best and find grace every day of your life. We don't know how long each of us have on earth. That's why we should see every day as a gift. If you do your part and I do my part, we can make this world a better place one day at a time.

It will take grace. It will take determination. It will take unity, and it will take mercy. I pray that God will bless, protect and keep you and your families for now and always.

CONTACT ME

Website: maryelizabethedwards.com
Email: edwards.maryelizabeth@gmail.com
Facebook: marytinyedwards

Made in the USA
Middletown, DE
03 November 2020